Tandie's Blues:
the Life Story of Tandie Klaasen

Published by ViVa Books
PO Box 23203, Claremont, 7735, South Africa

First published 1995
Reprinted 1996
Reprinted 2002
Reprinted 2005

ISBN 1 874932 22 0

Cover illustration by Lois Head

Acknowledgements
ViVa Books would like to thank Nedbank for their generous
contribution towards this book.

Photographic credits
Africa Photo News Service – Clifford Ranaka (page 42); Bailey's
African History Archives (opp. page 1, pages 2, 6, 8, 12, 13, 16, 18,
24, 27, 28, 29, 31, 32, 33, 34, 35, 37, 38, 40, 44, 47, 49, 50, 52, 53, 54,
55, 59, 60, 61, 64, 68, 69, 71, 72, 74, 75, 77, 79, 80, 81); London
Express News (page 36); Rogerio C. M. Pereira (page 51);
Tandie's personal photographs (pages 26, 30, 39, 45, 48, 67, 76);
Zonk magazine – courtesy Bona magazine (pages 21, 25, 41).

Reproduction by Remata Bureau and Printers, Midrand

Printed and bound by Mills Litho, Maitland, Cape Town, South Africa

Tandie's Blues:
the Life Story of
Tandie Klaasen

by Minky Schlesinger

Illustrated by Lois Head

x

Johannesburg

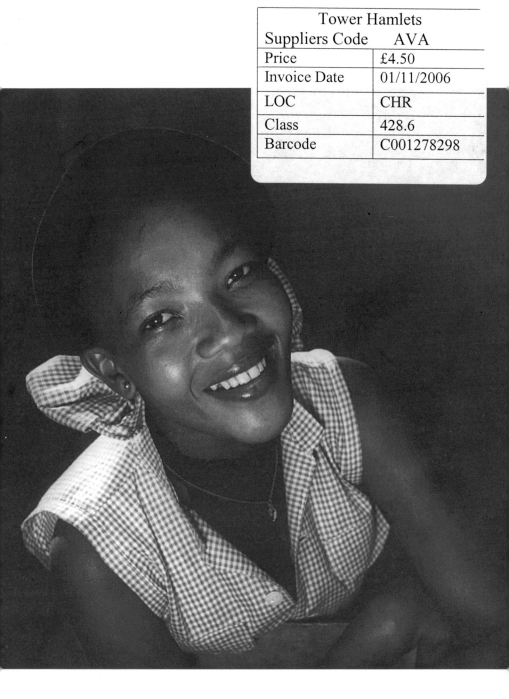

Chapter one
A child with stars in her eyes

Some books are about people who are famous. Other books are about people with a lot of talent. Tandie Klaasen is well known and talented. But she was not the biggest star of the 1950s. And she did not make a lot of money. Yet Tandie is special. Life gave her many hard knocks. Each time she picked herself up and carried on. Tandie has struggled through bad times with strength and courage. And that is why we tell her story.

Tandie's parents, William and Evelyn Mpambani, lived in Turffontein. During the late 1920s they were employed by a family called Van der Merwe. William worked in the Van der Merwes' butchery. And Evelyn worked in the kitchen.

Tandie was born on 27 September 1931. Shortly after her birth the Van der Merwes died. So Tandie's family moved to 18 Tucker Street in Sophiatown. There, William Mpambani had his own business. He fixed broken shoes.

Many great writers, musicians and politicians lived in Sophiatown. Many dangerous gangsters lived

Sophiatown, where Tandie grew up.

there too. One of these gangs was called the
Americans. They copied their style from gangsters
in American films. They wore fancy clothes, which
they bought or stole from shops in town. They
also liked to wear two-tone shoes made from good
leather. When the Americans' shoes were broken
they went to William Mpambani to get them fixed.
They called William 'Cuthberts'. That was the
name of an expensive shoe-shop in town. Tandie
says that everyone loved her father, especially the
Americans.

Tandie's mother, Evelyn, was a domestic worker.
Evelyn carried little Tandie, her first-born, on her
back while she swept the floors. But then Evelyn
had more children. William said that Evelyn must
stay at home to look after the babies. In the end
William and Evelyn had three daughters and nine
sons.

The Mpambanis lived in a three-roomed house.
There was a big dining-room where the family ate
their meals and relaxed. Evelyn and William slept
in one bedroom. And all the children shared
mattresses in the other room. Tandie says: 'We
couldn't bother how we slept. We just shared.'
They did not have much money and life was not
easy.

The Mpambanis were strict, God-fearing people. Tandie says: 'My father and my mother never drank alcohol or smoked. They were too straight with everything - too straight with my life.' Even though her parents were strict and money was short, Tandie was a happy child. She remembers that the family laughed a lot together. And they were always singing from the Bible or a songbook.

Both William and Evelyn had beautiful voices. On Sundays they went to the Methodist church. There they sang in praise of the Lord. Tandie remembers: 'The church service always started at half past six on Sunday morning. When we got there at eleven, everyone was singing so loudly you would think the roof was coming down. The congregation beat the Bibles in their hands to keep in time. Heads and shoulders swayed to the music ...'

One day in church Tandie sat next to a girl with a lovely singing voice. Everyone watched this young girl as the congregation sang 'Abide with Me'. Even in those early days Tandie wanted people to look at her. So Tandie sang louder and louder. Then she started shaking her head. But the church-members kept their eyes on the other

girl who sang so beautifully. Tandie began to sing
off-key. She wanted to spoil the other girl's tune.

Tandie's mother got cross. '*Haai*, Tandie!' she said.
'You mustn't do that!'

But Tandie did not care. Even now Tandie does
not care. She says: 'I would go back today and
block her again!'

This fighting spirit helped Tandie through many hard days. But it also got her into trouble. 'I was a very naughty child,' says Tandie. 'My parents wanted me to be a nurse, but I had my own ideas.'

Tandie's ideas were about music. From the age of twelve she ran off on Sundays to watch shows. Her parents did not know where she was. Tandie went to the Anadale Hall in Sophiatown. She paid two shillings to see groups like the Gay Gaieties and the Harlem Swingsters on stage.

The Harlem Swingsters.

Tandie also loved to watch the older girls in the audience. The big girls came with their boyfriends. They wore lovely clothes and smiled happily. 'When I grow up,' Tandie thought, 'I will be pretty and all the boys will like me too!' She saw how the big girls tap-danced and did the jitterbug jive. Tandie copied them. She was a fast learner and picked up the new steps quickly.

Sometimes the police came to Anadale Hall and broke up the show. They hit people with sticks and arrested them. Then Tandie would have to run for her life. A dancehall is not the right place for a kid who is only twelve!

Right through her school years Tandie dreamt about going on the stage. She was a child with stars in her eyes. Tandie went to St Cyprian's and also Western Native Township School. Whenever there was a school concert she tap-danced and performed in funny sketches. 'But,' Tandie says, 'in singing I was not too professional!'

One day the famous Zonk troupe came to the school to play for the pupils. Zonk was a variety show. The performers did comedy sketches and played American jazz. A woman named Emily Koenane was one of the Zonk stars. Emily was known as the blues queen of South Africa. When little Tandie Mpambani heard Emily sing the blues, she fell in love with her. Tandie knew that the blues would be her special style too. After that day Tandie tried to copy Emily's singing. She followed Emily everywhere.

Emily Koenane.

Then Tandie heard that Emily was forming a new group. One day Tandie saw Emily in Good Street. Tandie ran up to her idol. 'Emily, Emily,' Tandie shouted, 'I would like to sing with you! Can you teach me to sing?' Tandie gave Emily a tickey to pay for the lessons.

Emily smiled. *'Tsamaye, tsamaye, tsamaye,'* she laughed. She was telling Tandie to go away like a good little girl.

But Tandie carried on. 'One day you are going to hear from me, because I really love your singing. But I don't know how you sing to make a song like that ...'

Emily was a big star. She turned to the other people in the street. 'This child is boring me,' she said and walked off.

Tandie kept talking. 'You are going to hear from me, lady,' she called, as Emily walked away. Everyone agreed that Tandie was growing up too fast.

From a young age Tandie knew the importance of money. Her father taught her to watch her cash. Tandie remembers that William always walked from Sophiatown into the city. He never used the trams. 'I have got good strong legs,' he said, 'and I can save the sixpence tram-fare.'

As a child Tandie thought money could buy anything. She even tried to buy her way out of trouble at school. Tandie tells this story: 'I was often late for school. And I was afraid of the teacher's cane. One time the schoolmaster came to hit me. I took out a penny and said, "Teacher, don't hit me. I'm sorry I came late."

That made him more cross. He told me to stick out my hand. I had to obey. But when he slammed his cane down I put my hand between my legs. "It's sore, it's sore," I cried. The other children just laughed. You can't bribe a teacher not to cane you.'

Tandie stayed in school until Standard Six. These days Tandie says that she really needed her education. But in the 1940s life was hard for the Mpambanis. Tandie had to start earning her own money. She wanted a job on the stage, but singing jobs were hard to find. So, as a teenager, Tandie ran away and worked as a nanny. A Dutch family

employed Tandie. She had to look after their son.
They paid her ten pounds a month and gave her a
room to sleep in.

When Tandie's parents found out they were very
upset. Tandie was supposed to be in school. The
Mpambanis could see that their daughter would
never be a nurse. So Evelyn told her: 'Tandiwe, do
what you have to do.' Tandie answered: 'I will try
to do good, Mama.' Tandie left her job and went
back home.

But often the Mpambanis did not know where
their daughter was. Tandie never went back to

school. Sometimes she
sang at talent contests
at the Odin Cinema in
Good Street. At other
times she went to the
Rio Cinema in town.
Tandie would meet
her boyfriend on the
corner of Tucker
Street. Then they
would spend the
whole afternoon
watching films.

One night Tandie did not come home. Her parents called the police. They looked everywhere for her. But Tandie had a singing job. She had gone on tour with the Gay Gaieties!

The Gay Gaieties, before Tandie joined them.

The group was led by Mr J. P. Tutu. Tandie lied to Mr Tutu. She told him that her parents had given her permission to go on tour. When the Gay Gaieties came back to Johannesburg, Tandie was too scared to go home. So she went to Mr Tutu's house in Newclare.

But she could not stay away from home for ever. When at last Tandie did go back, her father was holding a big stick. He was ready to give Tandie a hiding. 'Where have you been?' he shouted.

'Look Tata, I was earning money,' Tandie answered quietly. She held out forty pounds. That was her pay for singing on tour.

William was surprised. He never knew that singing could bring in so much cash. But he did not want Tandie to go back on tour. 'Yo! Don't do this again. I will hit you!' William said.

Then Mr Tutu spoke to the Mpambanis. He told William and Evelyn that their daughter had a lot of talent. Mr Tutu said Tandie was behaving well. He would look after her while she was on stage. That was how Tandie got her first real singing job with the Gay Gaieties.

But after a while the Gay Gaieties split up. Tandie went back to domestic work. She was still just a teenager. Over the next years Tandie worked for different families. Some of her employers were hard and cruel. Others treated her well.

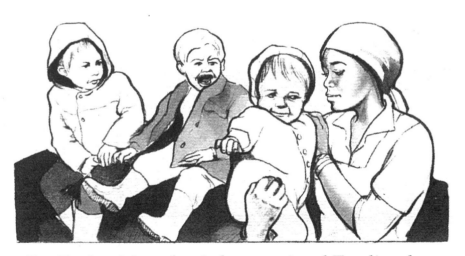

But Evelyn Mpambani always missed Tandie when she had a live-in job. She would go to Tandie and say: 'You are my daughter, you must come home. I can't sleep if you are not there.'

Tandie worked as a nanny during the day. But at night and on weekends she entered talent contests. One day during a contest at the Odin Cinema Tandie sang a song called 'Cow Cow Boogie'. The audience went crazy. Tandie won first prize for singing. Then she and her partner, Duba Duba, jived their way to the first prize for dancing.

Tandie was very lucky that day. Taai Shomang, the leader of the famous band the Harlem Swingsters, was in the audience. He invited Tandie to sing with his band. Tandie's career was starting to move!

Chapter two
The struggle for success

During the late 1940s Tandie's luck went up and down. She tried very hard to become a real star, but nothing lasted long. Tandie joined up with different bands, but she never stayed with any of them.

First of all, Tandie teamed up with Taai Shomang and the Harlem Swingsters. They performed old *marabi* tunes in the jazz style. Tandie sang 'Tamatie Sous' and 'Eggs and Toast' with the Swingsters and got the crowd jiving. But Tandie soon quarrelled with the band-members and left the group.

People told many stories about why Tandie quit. Jealous folk said Tandie was in love with the leader of the Swingsters, but he did not love her back. Tandie's enemies said she flirted with all the boys in the band at the same time. So they kicked her out. Tandie says the quarrel was about money. She says she did not get paid for her work. One thing is sure: there was a bad argument and Tandie left the band.

Tandie had many arguments in those days. She was not scared to speak out if she did not like something. A teenage girl is often shy. But not Tandie Mpambani!

A journalist told this story: It was 1948 and Tandie was just seventeen. She was singing her well-known 'Cow Cow Boogie' at a concert. Tandie was wearing blue jeans that made her look just like a boy. She wore a tight sweater. And she had a smart cap on her head.

Tandie sang her tune with a lot of bounce. She snapped her fingers, clapped her hands, jived and jumped. But the microphone was too short for Tandie. The audience could not hear her sing. In the middle of the song an actor called Toko Kampempe tried to lift Tandie's microphone. Tandie was not pleased. She frowned at Toko. Then she slapped the mike right out of his hands. Toko quickly got out of Tandie's way. People learned not to meddle with Miss Tandie Mpambani.

After Tandie left the Harlem Swingsters she sang for the Shantytown Sextet. But soon she was out on her own again. Her luck never lasted. One journalist wrote that Tandie complained to him again and again. She always said: 'Gee, why can't I be lucky too?'

But Tandie Mpambani was a fighter. She knew she had to make her own luck. She saw that it was bad to sing with male musicians. When she sang with men things ended up in a fight. Tandie looked around at the most famous township groups. The top groups all had four or five male vocalists, singing in close harmony. There were troupes like the African Inkspots and the Manhattan Brothers. They were township heroes.

Tandie decided to start her own vocal group. But Tandie's group would have only women in it. At that time Tandie was working as a domestic for a family called Cottam. The Cottams lived in Yeoville. Tandie's sister Tandeka was also working as a domestic, close by. Tandie asked Tandeka to sing lead vocals and the Quad Sisters were born.

Tandie says: 'Nobody thought there could be a female group at the time, but the Quad Sisters always stole the show. Besides Tandeka there were other great lady singers, like Joyce "Confess" Senaka and Stella Mbanze, and I was the fourth ... I think the others are all dead now.'

Tandie and the other women made up their own songs. They sang sad tunes about the hard things in life. And they also sang traditional tunes. They

Three of the Quad Sisters - Joyce Senaka, Tandie and Stella Mbanze.

had their first hit in 1952 with 'Carolina Wam', meaning 'My Carolina'. In 1953 they took the American tune 'Blue Moon' and wrote new words for it. The record was called 'Kulusizi', which means 'It's Tough Luck'. The flip side was 'Nda Ndinomfana', meaning 'I Had a Boyfriend'.

Tandie wrote sad songs about boyfriends because she had boyfriend trouble. As a teenager and in her early twenties Tandie went out with a gangster. His name was Cow Cow. You might think that he got his name from 'Cow Cow Boogie'. But Tandie says: 'His mother called him Cow Cow because he had a round face.'

Cow Cow was a pickpocket. Sometimes he and his gang went to the railway-yard and stole boxes of clothing from the goods trains.

Tandie says: 'Us girls would get a new jersey! They called us molls. It was a rough life.'

Cow Cow was very handsome. His clothes were smart and stylish. All the women fancied him. And Cow Cow liked the ladies. Tandie tells this story: 'Another woman, also named Thandi, had a love affair with Cow Cow behind my back. She was a shoplifter. One day I was in a restaurant in Smal Street. Thandi was there too. Someone told me about her and Cow Cow. I was fed up. I chased Thandi around the restaurant. She ran behind a counter, but she could not escape from me. I stabbed her!'

Tandie was lucky not to be arrested for this stabbing.

But Cow Cow kept playing around with other women. In 1954 Tandie landed up in jail because of Cow Cow. Tandie quarrelled with the film star Ribbon Dhlamini, because Ribbon was flirting with Cow Cow. They started fighting and Ribbon got stabbed. This time Tandie was arrested. Tandie lost the court case. She spent six months in jail.

Many black women served time in prison during the 1950s. There were pass laws, liquor laws and immorality laws that landed women in jail. But Tandie admits that she brought this trouble on her own head. She says: 'I was a rough woman. I wouldn't take no for an answer!'

Tandie carried·on singing with the Quad Sisters. Their records were big sellers in the townships. But Tandie and the other women never got any of that money. Sometimes the Quad Sisters did not even have bus-fare after they had made a record. They had to walk from the studio, in Booysens, all the way to town. While the singers were walking home, the record producer used to drive past them. He never stopped to give them a lift. He just waved and sped on.

The record company was supposed to pay the Quad Sisters money for every record they sold. This money is called a 'royalty'. But the company paid the women ten pounds each and nothing more. Tandie says: 'At first we didn't know we were being cheated. And when we found out, who could we talk to?' Young black female artists could not argue with a mighty record company in the 1950s.

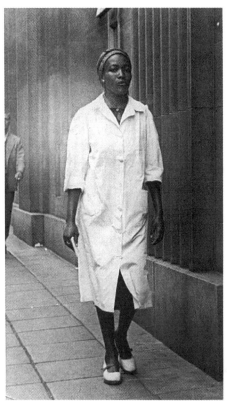

So Tandie kept working as a nanny for the Cottam family. That was how she earned steady money. And in her spare time she reached for the stars.

The Quad Sisters soon saw that they would never get rich from their singing. The record company cheated them. Concert promoters tricked them. Sometimes, after performing, the Sisters went home with no pay at all. In those days black women had little power. They struggled for every cent. After a few years the Quad Sisters broke up. The women thought they would try their luck separately.

Luck came quickly for Tandie. The Cuban Brothers needed a new singer. Miriam Makeba had been the Cubans' vocalist. But Miriam left them to sing with the Manhattan Brothers. Now the Cubans invited Tandie to take Miriam's place. So Tandie stepped into Miriam's shoes and teamed up with the Cuban Brothers.

Tandie with the Cuban Brothers.

In the mid-1950s Tandie and the Cuban Brothers joined the *African Jazz and Variety Show*. This show was put on by Alf Herbert, who was a white promoter. Herbert staged *African Jazz and Variety* at white theatres for white audiences. But he only

Alf Herbert with members of African Jazz and Variety.

employed black musicians, actors and dancers.
Herbert wanted to show white South Africans the
talent of black artists.

Tandie was very happy in the *African Jazz and
Variety Show*. She shared the stage with many
great artists. Dolly Rathebe, Dorothy Masuka,
Miriam Makeba and the Manhattan Brothers all
appeared in the show. *African Jazz and Variety*
played in Johannesburg for a long time. Then,
over the next few years, the troupe toured
throughout South Africa. Alf Herbert bought train
tickets for everyone, and Tandie got to see all the

big cities. Tandie swam in the sea in Durban. She shopped in Port Elizabeth. She had fun in Cape Town. Life was exciting.

The *African Jazz and Variety* team were very lively. They would do anything for a laugh. Tandie remembers that a friend called Pinnochio Mokaleng wanted to go to Cape Town. But he was short of cash. Pinnochio was the founder of the Modern

Martha Thetele and Tandie tickle Dolly Rathebe.

Jazz Club at the Odin Cinema in Sophiatown. Pinnochio was not in the *African Jazz and Variety* group. But when the show toured to Cape Town, the musicians smuggled Pinnochio onto the train with them. Nobody ever found out and Pinnochio had a good holiday. A few years later Pinnochio left South Africa to live in London.

Whenever Tandie went on tour her mother took over Tandie's job. Tandie did not want to lose her work at the Cottam family because it was regular money. A singer's earnings go up and down. The Cottams were quite happy for Evelyn to take Tandie's place for a while. The Cottams wanted to help Tandie to be a singer. They even drove Tandie to her singing jobs at night. Tandie remembers the Cottam family very fondly.

The mid-1950s were good years for Tandie. There was another reason why life looked so rosy. She had met a quiet young man named Lucas Klaasen.

By now Tandie was fed up with Cow Cow. He still chased after other women. Her parents had never liked Cow Cow. Tandie's father was very unhappy that she was learning gangster ways. So when Tandie met Lucas, the whole family was pleased.

Lucas Klaasen.

**Lucas and Tandie at the station before an
African Jazz and Variety tour.**

Lucas worked in a furniture factory. He was a
steady, stable person and he loved Tandie very
much. 'Anyway,' says Tandie, 'he was more
handsome than Cow Cow!' Many other women
used to look at Lucas. But Lucas warned them:
'You better leave me alone. My girlfriend is a
tigress and she will scratch you!'

Tandie and Lucas were married and the babies followed quickly. On 16 July 1955 Tandie gave birth to a son, Roger. And on 15 May 1957 she had a daughter. They named her Lorraine. Tandie says she was the happiest woman under the sun in those days.

Of course, nobody ever has only good things in their lives. The 1950s brought sad times too. In 1955 the government decided that Sophiatown should be for whites only. All the people living there were forced to move.

Tandie remembers how unhappy her family was to leave the place. She says: 'We loved Sophiatown. We stayed with Indians, Chinese and coloured

Everyone had to pack up and leave Sophiatown.

people. Our yard was owned by the Indians who lived there. We paid them rent. But they were just like family - we ate the Indian food, we called the old Indian lady "Mama". We were crowded in our three rooms. We didn't have taps. We had to get water from the pump. But it was home.

'Then one night the police came with big lorries - from Edward Street down to Anadale, over to Tucker Street. We had to load our things onto the lorry. Then they drove us to Meadowlands. Most of the people had never been to Soweto before.

Everything was new, with cement walls and cement floors. We lost so many friends. My father was crying. We were all crying. The lorry just threw us out and went back to collect more people from Sophiatown.' The Mpambanis finally got a house in Orlando in Soweto.

But good news was waiting just around the corner for Tandie. In the early 1960s she got her first trip overseas!

Chapter three

Tandie takes the plunge

Tandie's employers, the Cottams, were unhappy in South Africa. They hated the apartheid system. So the Cottams went to live in England. Tandie no longer had a steady job.

Tandie decided to take the plunge: she would try to be a full-time singer. She heard that the *King Kong* show needed new cast-members. *King Kong*, a musical play about a boxer, had been a big hit in South Africa. Now the show was touring to England. The producers wanted some fresh faces in the cast. Tandie auditioned and got a place on the tour!

Tandie waits to audition for King Kong.

In February 1961 Tandie packed her bags and kissed her family goodbye. She flew off with *King Kong* to sing and dance in England. It was a dream come true. The show opened at the Prince's Theatre in London. The first performance was a fancy affair. Many famous people were in the audience. Even Princess Margaret and her husband were there.

Londoners enjoyed the play. But it was not the same huge hit that it had been in South Africa. Even so, *King Kong* toured England for the whole of 1961.

Dambuza Mdledle, Peggy Phango and Little Lemmy Special with Princess Margaret and her husband.

Tandie and King Kong cast-members get a taste of English weather.

Tandie felt free in London. She stayed in a hotel for the first time. She shared a room with Abigail Bopape. Tandie and Abigail loved walking in the streets of London. Nobody asked them to show their passes because they were in town!

Tandie says: 'When I arrived in London I saw that everyone was learning music - black, white, and evergreen. Everything at home was for the whites. The schools were all for white people. Even if you had a lot of talent, you could not study music easily. Sometimes I wonder if I should have stayed overseas.'

Tandie makes a new friend.

Life in England was exciting. The cast saw all the sights of London. They made a number of new friends. There were wild parties after the show.

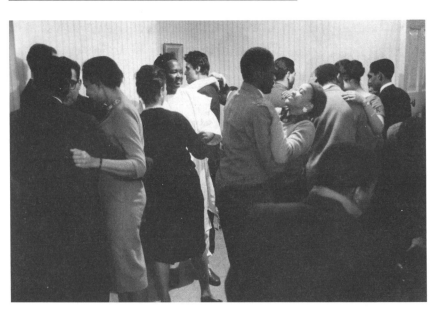

Many South Africans who lived in London came to see the play. They took the actors and actresses to fancy nightclubs. Tandie met up with her old friend Pinnochio Mokaleng and they showed the Londoners how to jive!

Tandie and Pinnochio.

Many members of the *King Kong* cast did not return home when the tour ended. They went into exile in England. But Tandie missed Lucas and her children badly. By Christmas of 1961 Tandie was

Lucas and Lorraine meet Tandie at the airport.

back with her family. Even though England was full of promise, Tandie would not go into exile.

Back in South Africa Tandie found that she was in demand. Now there were many musicals about township life. Everyone was trying to copy the success of *King Kong*. And they all wanted Tandie in their shows! She went straight into a play called *Mr Paljas* by Fred Engelen. Then Ben 'Satch' Masinga invited her to sing in *Back in Your Own Backyard*. This jazz musical was in Zulu. It played at the Bantu Men's Social Centre. After that Gibson Kente asked Tandie to be in his musical. It was called *Sikalo*. Kente's play was a sad story about the pain and sorrow of township life. Tandie had never been busier.

But, at that time, a lot of pain and sorrow came into Tandie's life too. Firstly, she had to tour to Cape Town and Durban with the shows. She spent much time away from her husband and children. Tandie knew that, as a performer, she would have to make this sacrifice for the rest of her life. 'I'll just have to look after them long-distance,' she said.

Tandie also suffered losses in her family. While she was in London her brother, Mzwandile, was

run over by a car in Soweto. Tandie was very
unhappy that she could not come home to bury
him. Then, after Tandie got back, her father passed
away. Tandie's mother took these deaths badly.
Evelyn's health was not good after that.

Tandie had to attend many funerals.

Before the family finished mourning there was
another death. This time Tandie's favourite
brother, Boy, was hanged for murder. Boy had
killed a policeman. Some people remember that
the policeman was shot during a bank robbery.
But they say that Boy did not pull the trigger.
Other people remember that Boy hit a policeman

who wanted to see his pass. In any case, in 1962 Boy went to the gallows.

Tandie tells this story: 'The night before the hanging I slept on the pavement outside the jail. In the early morning I heard my brother singing. He was trying to be brave. I asked the priest to tell Boy I was there. I also started to sing. I knew Boy could hear me. We sang together like that, him inside the jail and me on the pavement.

'Then a white man walked past with his dog. The dog went for me. There was blood all over the pavement. The man helped me to clean myself up.

'He said: "Lady, this dog never bites. Something terrible is going to happen to you."

'I answered, "Yes, today is the day my brother is going to be hanged."'

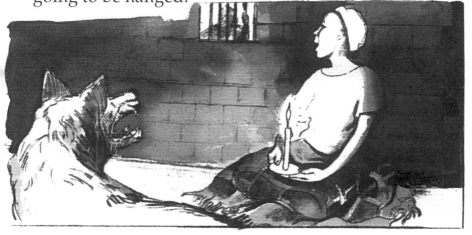

This came to be the pattern of Tandie's life. Whenever things were going well for her, bad luck was not far away.

During the mid-1960s Tandie teamed up again with Alf Herbert and *African Jazz and Variety*. Herbert had changed the show. He cut the cast down to half its size. He employed the sexiest women around. Then he dressed them in skimpy costumes, showing a lot of naked flesh. He knew that many white men would pay good money to see these sexy women.

Alf Herbert arranged for *African Jazz and Variety* to tour Australia and New Zealand. He changed the name of the show to the *African Follies*. He put in new acts for overseas audiences. One new act showed Shaka's murder. Another sketch showed 'tribes'

Tandie in the new African Jazz and variety.

killing a person as an offering to God. Herbert put in a sexy python dance and a lot of bare-breasted women. He knew what foreign audiences wanted!

A few days before Tandie flew to Australia, bad luck knocked on her door again. Little Lorraine, who was now eight years old, was playing at the Klaasens' house in Thokoza. Lorraine hid away in a big cardboard box. Some other children found the box. They

Lorraine Klaasen.

did not see that Lorraine was inside it. The children set the box on fire. Neighbours heard

Lorraine screaming and pulled her out. Lorraine was badly burnt. She spent many months in the Natalspruit Hospital.

Tandie could not cancel the Australian tour. So she got on the plane with a heavy heart. She had left Lorraine in the hospital. Performers always say 'the show must go on'. Many times Tandie sang and danced while her heart was breaking.

In Australia Tandie felt that the other women in the show did not like her. Tandie says: 'They would be in groups and they would talk about me.

Some of the women in African Jazz and Variety.

But I would go out and meet Australians. I couldn't be bothered with the other girls. Alf Herbert said I was unfriendly because I wouldn't go to the parties. He told people that he couldn't stand me. But he needed me in the show.'

When the tour was over Tandie had a real treat. The cast sailed back to South Africa on a ship! Tandie had a wonderful rest and made many new

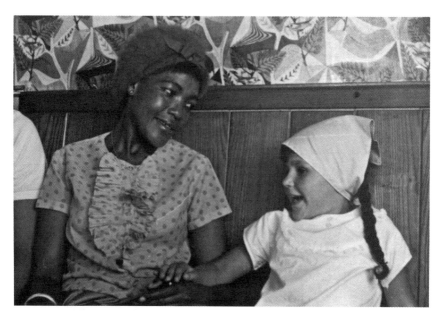

friends. She had a special friendship with a little white girl. Tandie gave her the nickname 'Tandeka'.

When Tandie got home she was again in demand. But not as an actress in a play or in a variety show. Now Tandie was in demand as a solo cabaret artist. Nightclubs throughout the country invited Tandie to sing and entertain their guests. Tandie performed at fancy places like Ciro's and the Cellar in Durban. She sang in clubs in Johannesburg and Cape Town, and she was popular at the Swaziland Spa. Tandie also did regular shows at the Holiday Inn hotels. She was never short of work.

Tandie had to leave Lorraine behind when she performed in other towns.

When Tandie was not singing in clubs, she
performed at large open-air jazz festivals. She
shared the stage with big names like Kippie
Moeketsi, Winston 'Mankunku' Ngozi, the
drummer Early Mabuza and singer Sophie Mgcina.

Tandie's career really started to hot up in 1970.
Tandie was singing at a nightclub in Maputo in
Mozambique. In those days Maputo was called
Lourenço Marques. It was a smart city with
beautiful beaches and a busy night-life. Many
wealthy South Africans used to go there on
holiday. Tandie sang with the Chris Schilder Trio.

Tandie and the Chris Schilder Trio in Mozambique.

She was now an experienced singer. She could handle all kinds of songs. She told jokes well, and the audiences loved her.

Then, in August 1970, American soul-singer Percy Sledge toured South Africa. He chose two supporting singers. One of them was Stella Starr. And the other was Tandie Klaasen! When they performed together at the Eyethu Cinema in Soweto, the audience clapped until their hands ached. Tandie says that the people liked her too much. 'After the first performance Percy Sledge

52

cut my act to two songs. He thought I got too much applause.'

Life got better and better. In December 1971 American singer Eartha Kitt visited this country. Eartha was booked to sing at the Swaziland Spa. Tandie was also at the Swaziland Spa.

Percy Sledge kisses Tandie while Stella Starr smiles.

She was doing a cabaret show there. After Eartha finished her own show, she went along to listen to Tandie sing.

Tandie was shaking because she knew Eartha was there. Tandie dedicated the 'Click Song' to Eartha. But Eartha did not clap, she just sat there quietly. Then Tandie did her last song, 'I Who Have Nothing'. When Tandie finished singing Eartha clapped louder and longer than anyone else. She

Tandie with Eartha Kitt.

thought Tandie was great. The two women went off to the Penguin nightclub together.

A concert promoter from Japan was at the Swaziland Spa that weekend. He saw Eartha and Tandie perform. The promoter invited Tandie to go to Japan. He wanted her to do a show with the singer Nina Simone. At first Tandie did not believe him. But a few weeks later the promoter sent a letter. He had organized the tour. The promoter offered Tandie many thousands of rands if she would come to Japan.

Tandie was more excited than she had been in years. She went back to Thokoza and prepared for the trip. She told everyone about her good fortune. She would be leaving for Japan in October 1973. Tandie hoped this would be her big international break.

But Tandie had forgotten how bad luck followed her. In the next few weeks something happened that changed her life for ever.

Chapter four
Fire!

Tandie never went to Japan. Her big chance was ruined by a close friend.

At that time Tandie was living happily in Thokoza with her husband Lucas and daughter Lorraine.

Lorraine helps Tandie to cook a meal.

Tandie's son, Roger, lived with Tandie's mother. Roger was the darling of the Mpambanis. He even took the name Mpambani instead of Klaasen. So Roger stayed with his grandmother.

In Thokoza Tandie had a friend named Irene Bowes. Irene lived nearby. Whenever Tandie went overseas Irene looked after Lorraine. Tandie says, 'Irene was my dear friend and I loved her.'

Irene was a shebeen queen. She always nagged Tandie to bring famous musicians and white friends to her shebeen. Tandie did not like it when people tried to use her fame. But Tandie and Irene got on very well together.

On 11 August 1973, two months before Tandie was leaving for Japan, Irene came to Tandie's house. Irene invited Tandie to have supper with her that night. Irene said she would cook roast beef and dumplings. She kissed Tandie on the forehead and said, 'I'll see you tonight!' Then Irene left.

That evening Tandie went to Irene's house with a happy heart. Her future looked good and she felt fine. Tandie did not know that her life was in danger.

Tandie tells the story: 'When I got to Irene's gate, two young men were standing there. I knew them well. Their names were Willem and Theo. I had watched these two boys grow up from when they were kids.

'I saw Willem was hiding something under his jacket. I hoped he hadn't stolen something from

Irene. Inside the house they were playing my LP
Love is Strange.

'Suddenly I heard Irene shout "Haak!" That means
"now is the time!" Before I could see what was
going on, my head felt wet. Then I heard a loud
"Boom!" Something exploded on my face. Willem
and Theo had poured petrol over my head and lit a
match. I was on fire!

'I didn't believe it was me. I was fighting with this fire. My flesh was falling off my hands and face. I was screaming, "My God, it's me!" Doom, doom, doom! I could hear the sound of fire on me. My head was as heavy as a rock. I couldn't believe what I was seeing - it was me.

'Willem's brother was there. He threw his jacket on me and pulled me into the street. I hit a rock and my two front teeth cut into my tongue. Someone rushed off to call my sister Tandeka, who was at my place with Lorraine. The two of them came running. Lorraine tried to beat the flames off me. She burnt her hands and legs. People told me she fainted.'

Tandie was taken to the Natalspruit Hospital. As soon as the nurses saw Tandie, they put her in a bath of cold water. Everyone was upset that the well-known singer was so badly burnt. The nurses dressed Tandie's wounds. Then they gave her a bed in a quiet room, away from the other patients. Tandie says: 'I was on the fifth floor of the hospital because of the smell. I smelt like a dead person. I used to sleep with my fingers blocking my nose.'

Tandie's face, neck and hands were covered in bandages. Nobody knew how she would look

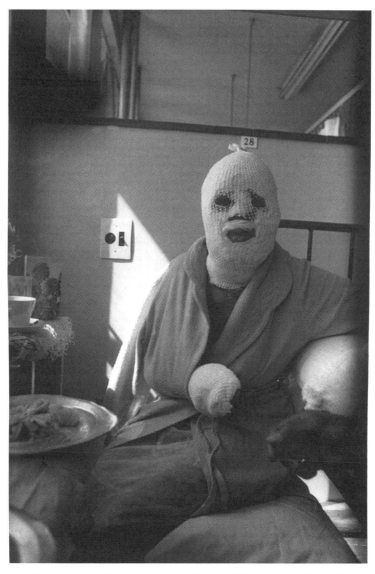

after the wounds were healed. Tandie told the doctors, 'I'm going to kill myself if I don't see my face!' But it was too early to take the bandages off.

Tandie's wounds itched. She felt as if red ants were crawling over her. Her face was as hard as a rock under the bandages. She did not know if she wanted to live or die.

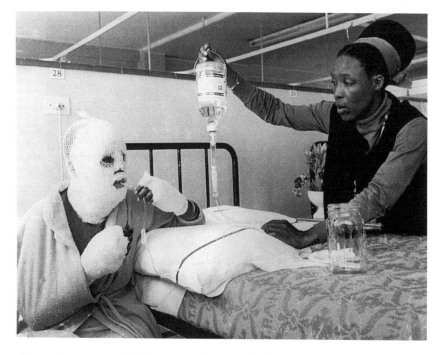

Tandie says: 'When, at last, the bandages came off, the doctors were worried. They didn't know how I was going to take it. They had an injection needle ready just in case. When the nurse folded back the dressing the smell was so strong. They took the bandage off and my flesh fell from it. One young doctor was trying not to cry.

'When I saw myself I understood his tears. My flesh was just hanging like a melted candle. Or when you go into a cave and see those stalactites. My skin looked like that. My neck was blown up. One muscle held my chin up. There was no mouth, just a hole. How would I ever sing again? I thought, "Lordy, take me now!"'

Tandie had four operations to build up her mouth. She had another operation on her neck. The doctors cut skin from Tandie's thigh. Then they sewed the skin onto her face. After that Tandie had to sleep standing up. The nurses tied Tandie to a support so that she would not fall over. While Tandie was in hospital she got many cards and flowers. But some of her show business friends did not visit her.

Tandie says: 'Some of the other lady singers were pleased that this happened to me. They were jealous of me. Now they said I was finished. They said my career was over.' Tandie read stories in the newspapers that she would never sing again.

When Tandie got back home things did not get better. Tandie had been a beautiful woman and now she was hardly recognizable. Many members of the community could not look at her. She was rejected by old friends and neighbours. Even Lucas Klaasen no longer wanted Tandie next to him. Lorraine begged him, 'Daddy, don't leave now when Mommy needs us most.' But Lucas could not live with Tandie. Tandie says it was because she was too ugly. Lucas walked out after sixteen years of marriage. Tandie was left alone with Lorraine.

On 13 December 1973 Willem Alberts was charged in court for assaulting and trying to murder Tandie. Theo, the other boy, was never caught. Willem was found guilty. He was sentenced to three years in prison. When Willem saw Tandie in court he fainted. Tandie asked him, 'Why?' But Willem had no answer.

Everyone wanted to know why Willem did such a
thing. Tandie says: 'Irene Bowes's son told us that
it was Irene's fault. He heard Irene and Willem
planning to burn me.' Some people say that Irene
quarrelled with Tandie about a man. Other people
say that Irene was envious of Tandie's success.
Tandie says she thinks Irene might have been
jealous. But she is not sure to this day why her
friend turned against her.

In the next few months Tandie started drinking
alcohol to ease her pain. She could not believe
what had happened to her. She had lost her

beauty, her husband, and her health in a few short weeks. People were whispering that Tandie had also lost her career. They said she was finished.

Tandie says: 'I was so hurt. But the more hurt I feel, the stronger I get. I am God's child. I prayed, "Lord, you know, just pave the way for me. I mean, I'm a sinner, but I'm still your child. I'm your daughter. Where I've gone wrong, forgive me." I was not finished. Even through my pain and suffering I knew it. Faith can move mountains. This was not the end of Tandie Klaasen.'

Chapter five
Still going strong

Tandie had to rebuild her whole life. Luckily, she had two very good friends who cared about her. Juliet Abel and David Lewis from the Holiday Inn hotels helped Tandie to get back on her feet. Juliet and David could not employ Tandie as a cabaret artist at the hotels any more. Audiences wanted to watch pretty women sing. Tandie's skin was stretched tight across her face. She had holes and scars on her neck. Tandie's looks would not help her to get jobs.

Tandie says: 'Juliet Abel was my agent at that time. She was a wonderful woman. She bought me groceries while my wounds were healing.' David Lewis gave Tandie one hundred rands each month for six months after the attack. In 1973 a person could live quite well on one hundred rands a month. So Tandie did not have to worry about earning a living. She put all her power into getting her life right again.

Tandie's first task was to stop drinking. Slowly and with great strength Tandie came off the bottle. These days Tandie drinks alcohol at parties, or when she is relaxing with friends. But she does not look in a bottle for courage. Tandie worries about some of the young singers today who are always drunk. She tells young artists, 'Look, sister, if I can give up the booze after all my troubles, you can do it too!'

Tandie's next step was to get back on the stage again. She had always loved singing the blues. Since Tandie's school-days when she heard Emily Koenane sing, she felt drawn to the blues.

Blues music was sung in America by slaves, many years ago. In those days slave-traders used to catch people in Africa. They took these people to America and sold them there as slaves. The slaves worked long and hard picking cotton and doing other heavy work in the southern part of America. They sang songs full of pain and loneliness. This music came to be known as the 'blues'.

Tandie had also learnt what suffering was. She also knew pain and loneliness. Now she sang with even more passion and feeling. Tandie says: 'Blues is something you feel inside yourself that you want to express to people. The words of one of my best songs go: "My man don't love me, he treats me awful mean ..." Sometimes you want to talk about things like that and people are in a hurry. They don't want to listen. But when you're on stage people have paid their money to listen. They're not in a hurry to go. I can pour out all my blues. Nobody will walk away.'

Less than a year after she was burnt Tandie stepped onto the stage again. She appeared in July 1974 at the Sound Power Jazz Festival at the Jabulani Amphitheatre. The Master of Ceremonies was the famous actor, Ken Gampu.

Ken put his arm gently around Tandie and led her onto the stage. There were thousands of people in the audience. At first Tandie did not want to look up at them. She was scared her fans would reject her.

Then Tandie took the microphone. The audience was dead silent. Tandie started to sing. She sang, 'The first time ever I saw your face, I thought the sun rose in your eyes ...' Many fans started to weep. By the end of the song Tandie was also weeping. The audience stood up and cheered her. They still loved Tandie and they told her so.

After that it was easier for Tandie to appear on stage again. Many people were very kind. Queeneth Ndaba, who was a dress designer and a promoter, organized a big show at the Eyethu Cinema in Soweto. The show raised funds for Tandie. Tandie needed a lot of money to pay for all the operations and medicines.

But not everyone was kind. Tandie did a fund-raising concert in Durban at the Orient Hall. The hall could hold seven hundred people. But only one hundred music lovers came. Tandie was

Tandie dresses for a concert.

very hurt. She told a newspaper: 'I gave my best for this city, its nightclub owners, its people, its promoters. I need them today but they keep away from me.' Tandie sang her heart out that evening. And the small audience would not let her go. They kept Tandie on stage until long after midnight.

Slowly Tandie got used to her new face. And her fans got used to the new Tandie. By 1976 Tandie was ready to appear in a musical play again. Des and Dawn Lindberg gave her a lead role in their new show. It was called *The Black Mikado*.

The Lindbergs also offered Lorraine a part in *The Black Mikado*. Lorraine was now nineteen. Over the years she had become a talented singer and dancer. For the first time Tandie and her daughter shared the stage together. Many newspapers wrote that Tandie was the best thing in the show.

That year Tandie won the Count Pushkin Award for being the best female vocalist of the year. Life was improving. But, as always for Tandie, things started to go sour. Before long Tandie and the Lindbergs quarrelled about money. Tandie felt she was not being paid enough for her work. Tandie and Lorraine found themselves out of the show.

Tandie and Ben 'Satch' Masinga in the Black Mikado.

Throughout her career Tandie felt that people were cheating her. She also often felt that other artists were against her. Tandie says: 'The other lady singers were not happy that I won the Count Pushkin Award. They thought I was done a favour. Not one of them came to congratulate me.' Tandie never felt well liked. The only time she was sure that people liked her, was when she sang on-stage. When the audiences cheered, Tandie felt happy and loved.

And audiences still wanted to hear Tandie sing. Over the next few years Tandie and Lorraine performed wherever they could. They did shows

Lorraine and Tandie.

at clubs, hotels and festivals. Tandie proved that a woman did not have to be a beauty queen to please an audience.

In the early 1980s Tandie and Lorraine travelled together to Israel. They did a show there called *Sola Sola*. Tandie says that people were very kind in Israel. The Israelis asked Tandie to visit some hospitals. She spoke to people who were suffering from burns. Tandie told the patients her story. She told them that their lives were not over. They were not finished.

On the way home from Israel, Tandie and Lorraine visited a Greek island. There they met a young man named Ignace Lumumba, who was a student. Ignace was a nephew of the late Congolese leader, Patrice Lumumba. Ignace's mother lived in Montreal in Canada.

Tandie could see that Ignace and Lorraine liked each other a lot. The Greek island was beautiful and romantic. The two young people spent lazy, happy days together. Soon they were deeply in love. Before long Ignace asked Lorraine to marry him. Lorraine would have to go and live in Canada with the Lumumba family. Tandie was to lose her beloved daughter.

Tandie still misses Lorraine terribly. But she goes to Canada to visit her often. The Lumumbas have two daughters. Tandie loves to take special gifts from Africa for her grandchildren.

For the past eight years Lorraine has had her own show in Canada. She and her group sing and dance all the old South African styles. These days the show is called *Soweto Groove*. Lorraine and her group have toured all over Canada, to Holland and to some cities in America. Whenever Tandie goes to Montreal she joins Lorraine's show as a guest artist. In 1986 Tandie toured with them in Montreal, Ottawa and New York City. The American papers wrote that Tandie was like Ella Fitzgerald.

After Lorraine left the country, Tandie started to lose many of the people she loved. In 1983 Tandie's mother Evelyn died.

Tandie and her mother Evelyn with her friends, in younger days.

Tandie's sister, Tandeka.

A couple of years later Tandie's sister Tandeka, who had been in the Quad Sisters, was killed by thugs in Zola. One by one her brothers and sisters passed away, until only one brother remained. And Tandie does not see eye to eye with him.

Luckily there are nephews around and Tandie gets on well with them. Tandie's son Roger has also stayed in South Africa. Roger married a young nurse named Nomhle. Tandie says: 'I have a very nice daughter-in-law. But I leave them to get on with their lives. Children need that.'

Tandie has lost a great deal over the years. As we get older we all lose our youth and beauty. All of us must say goodbye to loved ones. But Tandie lost too many things too early in life. She is not bitter. But she has a deep sadness inside her. She also has great strength.

One thing Tandie refused to lose was her singing career. It is not the career of a superstar. Tandie never made much money. The chance to be a superstar was taken away twenty years ago, when Tandie was turned into a human torch. But she has never given up. Tandie is too stubborn for that. She is still in demand throughout the country.

Over the past years Tandie has appeared with all the best bands and singers. She sang with the Afro-jazz group Bayete. She did a show called *Two-Tone* in Durban with Jenny da Lenta. When there were Jazz festivals at Fun Valley and Jabulani, they always invited Tandie to be in the line-up. The Music Platform at the Market Theatre in Johannesburg asked Tandie to appear with Abigail Kubheka and Sam Marais. At the People's Music Festival organized by the United Democratic Front, Tandie was introduced as 'the Queen of them all'.

In recent years Tandie has sung at nightclubs like Club 58, the Black Sun and Club Kilimanjaro, all in Johannesburg. She was asked to perform at the wedding of Zinzi Mandela, daughter of the President. Tandie has done fund-raising concerts at Johannesburg's Civic Theatre. She is also a regular at Kippie's Jazz Club. Tandie may not be a superstar, but she remains a working singer.

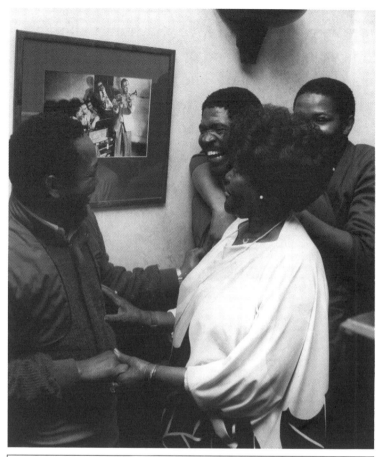

Tandie and Hugh Masekela at Kippie's Jazz Club.

And she can still hold an audience in the palm of her hand. When she sings, her face relaxes. Tandie's warmth and courage shine through. Tandie says: 'Whether life is bad, hard, sad, humiliating or anything else, you have to learn to love yourself. You have to love yourself more than anything.' On stage Tandie is beautiful.

Tandie sings about lost love. She sings about friends who have passed on. She sings about the man she hopes to find. The burns have healed, but Tandie still feels the pain deep in her soul. Everyone listens when Tandie Klaasen sings the blues.

Word list

affair (page 36) - event

agent (page 65) - manager

applause (page 52) - clapping and cheering from an audience

arguments (page 18) - disagreements between two people

assaulting (page 62) - attacking

audience (pages 6, 16, 19 ...) - people watching a show

auditioned (page 35) - tried out for a part in the play

cabaret (pages 48, 52, 65) - singing and dancing

career (pages 16, 50, 62 ...) - working life

concert promoters (page 26) - people who put up the money for a concert

Congolese (page 73) - person who comes from the Congo

congratulate (page 72) - offer good wishes and praise

congregation (page 4) - church members

courage (pages 1, 66, 79) - bravery; strength

dressed (pages 44, 58, 69) - put medicine and bandages on

dumplings (page 56) - little balls made of dough

Dutch (page 11) - people from Holland

envious (page 63) - jealous

experienced (page 51) - skilled

favourite (page 42) - most loved

fed up (pages 23, 30) - very angry

foreign (page 45) - overseas

founder (page 29) - he started the Jazz Club

gallows (page 43) - place where people are hung

hardly recognizable (page 62) - people could not see who she was

humiliating (page 79) - shaming or humbling

idol (page 9) - famous person who is loved and admired

in demand (pages 40, 48, 78) - very popular

international (page 54) - all over the world

island (page 73) - small piece of land in the middle of the sea

jitterbug jive (page 7) - a wild dance

loneliness (page 66) - feeling of being alone or sad

love affair (page 23) - sexual relationship

make this sacrifice (page 41) - give up time with her family

Master of Ceremonies (page 67) - person who introduces the singers at a concert

microphone, mike (pages 19, 68) - a thing that picks up a singer's voice to make it louder

molls (page 22) - gangsters' girlfriends

nightclub (pages 39, 48, 50) - places where people go listen to music and dance

off-key (page 5) - out of tune

passion (page 66) - strong feelings

penny (page 11) - coin worth one cent

performed (pages 8, 17, 48 ...) - acted, sang or danced for an audience

permission (page 13) - agreed that she could go

politicians (page 1) - people who take part in government

professional (page 8) - like somebody who sings for a living

quarrelled (pages 17, 24, 63, 70) - fought

record producer (page 25) - person in charge of making records

regular (pages 30, 48, 78) - steady

rejected (page 62) - turned away

ruined (page 55) - spoiled

see eye to eye (page 76) - does not get on well

shoplifter (page 23) - person who steals things from shops when no one is looking

sixpence (page 10) - coin worth five cents

sketch (pages 8, 44) - short stories acted out on stage

stalactites (page 61) - long, hanging rocks inside a cave

stubborn (page 78) - persistent; needing to carry on

studio (page 25) - building where a record is made

superstar (pages 77, 78) - very famous and rich singer

takes the plunge (page 35) - tries something new

talent (pages 1, 12, 15 ...) - the ability to do something very well

talent contest (pages 12, 16) - competition for young singers and dancers

task (page 65) - duty or job

ten pounds (pages 12, 25) - twenty rands, in those days

tickey (page 9) - coin worth two and a half cents

traditional (page 20) - African tunes